Cracking Up
on April Fools
Volume 1

While every precaution has been taken in the preparation of this book, the publisher assumes no responsibility for errors or omissions, or for damages resulting from the use of the information contained herein.

CRACKING UP ON APRIL FOOLS VOLUME 1

First edition. October 4, 2023.

Copyright © 2023 Mar Ziq.

ISBN: 979-8223719946

Written by Mar Ziq.

A collection of hilarious
April Fools' Day jokes,
stand-up comedy, and
funny short stories.

Man: Did you hear about the invisible man who married an invisible woman?

Girl: No, what happened?

Man: Their kids were nothing to look at! (both laugh)

Girl: (rolling her eyes) That was terrible.

INTRODUCTION

Hello and welcome to the world of "Cracking Up on April Fools: A collection of hilarious April Fools' Day jokes, stand-up comedy, and funny short stories" volume 1. This book is a treasure trove of humor and wit, designed to tickle your funny bone and leave you in stitches.

From hilarious jokes to clever stand-up comedy routines, this book is packed with humor that will keep you entertained for hours. Whether looking for a good laugh, a quick pick-me-up, or just a little bit of silly fun, "Cracking Up on April Fools" has covered you.

This book has a lot of different kinds of humor, which is one of its best features. Whether you prefer witty one-liners or elaborate puns, you're sure to find something that will make you chuckle. This book is full of recent stories delivered through jokes and cartoon illustrations, making it a perfect choice for anyone who loves a good laugh.

One of the book's highlights is its collection of April Fools' jokes. April Fools' Day is a time-honoured tradition that many people look forward to each year, and this book has some of the best jokes around. You'll find everything from classic pranks to modern-day hijinks, all guaranteed to put a smile on your face.

But that's not all - "Cracking Up on April Fools" also features a variety of stand-up comedy routines, all centred around the theme of April Fools' Day. Some of the funniest comedians perform these routines, and they're sure to have you in stitches. Whether you're a fan of observational humor, satire, or good old-fashioned silliness, there's something here for everyone.

In addition to the April Fools' jokes and stand-up routines, this book also contains a selection of funny short stories. These stories are perfect for anyone who loves to curl up with a good book and lose themselves in a world of humor and wit. Each story is carefully crafted to deliver maximum laughs, which will leave you feeling entertained and amused.

But its approach to humor really sets "Cracking Up on April Fools" apart. This book isn't just about making you laugh - it's about exploring the funny side of life and seeing the humor in everyday situations. Whether you are stuck in traffic, dealing with a problematic coworker, or just feeling down, "Cracking Up on April Fools" will lift your spirits and put a smile on your face.

Finally, let's talk about the illustrations. Each joke and story is accompanied by charming cartoon illustrations, adding a layer of fun and humor to the book—the images are expertly drawn and perfectly capture the spirit of each joke and story.

In conclusion, "Cracking Up on April Fools" is a must-read for anyone who loves a good laugh. It's packed with humor, from clever jokes to hilarious stand-up routines to funny short stories. And with its charming illustrations and witty writing, it's sure to keep you entertained and amused for hours on end.

CHAPTER 1

The Art of Deception

A person is trying to teach their dog how to play dead. The dog is confused and says,

"I don't understand. I thought the whole point of being a dog was to be alive and play."

Story # 1

April Fools' Jokes:

Joke 1: "Even though I don't have dogs, I'll place a "Beware of the Dog" sign in my yard on April 1. That should stop the annoying neighbours and salespeople."

Joke 2: I will switch all the labels in my friend's pantry this year. Imagine their surprise when they think they're grabbing a bag of chips, but it's a bag of flour! Hilarious, right?

Joke 3: I'm going to hide my roommate's phone charger on April Fools' Day. I'll watch as they desperately search for it, only to realize it was in plain sight the whole time. The little things are what make life fun.

April Fools' Day stand-up comedy:

Thank you, thank you, thank you, it's great to be here tonight! So, April Fools' Day, the art of deception, huh? I must admit; I love a good prank as much as the next person. But you know what they say? The difference between a good and a nasty joke is about 20 years in prison.

Seriously, though, I've been thinking about April Fools' Day, and it's a weird holiday. I mean, think about it. We spend the other 364 days of the year telling people to be honest and trustworthy, and then on this one day, we're like, "Nah, just kidding, lie your ass off!"

And let's be honest; the art of deception is not for everyone—some people need to gain the skill set for it. My dad, for example, tried to prank me one year by telling me he had gotten me tickets to a Justin Bieber concert. And I was like, "And I responded, "Dad, you know I'm not 13 years old anymore;" I added, "Come on!"

But you know who is good at deception? Advertisers. Have you ever seen those fast-food commercials where the burger looks like a work of art, and then you go to the restaurant and get something that looks like it's been run over by a truck? That's some severe deception right there.

And keep me from getting started on social media. Have you ever responded, "Really?" to someone posting on social media about their unique life, relationships, and children? Because I saw you at the grocery store last week, you looked like you hadn't slept in three days."

But you know what? I have a confession to make. I love April Fools' Day, not for the pranks but for the sheer joy of watching people fall for them. There's something so satisfying about seeing someone get fooled, especially when you know they'll never live it down. And let's be honest here: all of us could use a good laugh right now.

So, in conclusion, if you're going to participate in April Fools' Day, remember to keep it light, keep it funny, and for the love of all that is holy, don't get yourself arrested. Thank you, and goodnight!

Story # 2

It was April Fools' Day, and the town of Whoville was buzzing with excitement. The mayor had announced a contest for the best April Fools' prank, and everyone was eager to show off their skills.

One man named Joe had always prided himself on being a master of deception. He had spent weeks planning the ultimate prank that would go down in Whoville history.

On the morning of April 1st, Joe put his plan into action. He went to the town square and set up a fake newsstand with a sign that read "Free April Fools' Day Prank Ideas." People gathered around, eager to see what Joe had in store.

As they approached the stand, Joe handed each person a slip of paper with a prank idea on it. Some were harmless, like pretending to spill a drink on someone. Others were more elaborate, like faking a car accident or a house fire.

The people of Whoville were impressed with Joe's creativity and he basked in their admiration. But as the day wore on, things started to turn dark. People began to carry out the pranks and chaos ensued.

The harmless pranks quickly turned into dangerous stunts, with people getting hurt and property getting damaged. The town was in disarray, and Joe realized he had made a grave mistake.

He tried to stop the madness, but it was too late. The damage had been done, and the people of Whoville were furious. They chased Joe out of town, vowing never to trust him again.

As he walked away, Joe couldn't help but think that maybe there was such a thing as taking April Fools' Day too far. From then on, he decided to stick to harmless pranks - like putting whoopee cushions on chairs and fake spiders in people's coffee cups. Because, you know, an excellent belly laugh is therapeutic.

The end.

Story # 3

April Fools' Jokes:

1. I decided to prank my coworkers by putting a sign on the elevator that read, "Voice-activated elevator: say the floor you want to go to." Watching them yell out their desired floors while I pressed the buttons from outside the elevator was hilarious.

2. I told my significant other I had booked a surprise trip to Hawaii for April Fools' Day. They were ecstatic until I revealed we were going to a fake beach in the middle of the city, with sand and palm trees.

Funny Short Story:

It was April Fools' Day, and the residents of the small town of Larksville were preparing for their annual prank war. For weeks, everyone had been coming up with elaborate schemes to outdo each other and earn the title of "King or Queen of Deception."

On the morning of April 1st, the town was bustling with activity. The baker had replaced the filling in his doughnuts with mustard, the local car dealership was offering free car washes that turned out to be buckets of water thrown on unsuspecting customers, and the town square was covered in fake dog poop.

But one person in Larksville was determined to win the prank war once and for all. His name was Tommy, and he was known throughout the town as the ultimate trickster. He had spent months planning his masterpiece, a prank so elaborate and devious that it would go down in history.

Tommy's plan involved rigging the town's water tower to spew out green dye when the water was turned on. He had spent countless hours sneaking into the building at night and installing the necessary equipment, all while evading the watchful eye of the town's sheriff.

As the day wore on, the pranks continued to escalate. People were being fooled left and right, and the air was filled with laughter and cheers. But Tommy bided his time, waiting for the perfect moment to unleash his masterpiece.

Finally, as the sun began to set, Tommy made his move. He snuck into the water tower and turned on the dye, watching with glee as the water turned green and began to flow out of the taps and showers throughout the town.

At first, people were amused by the sudden change in color, thinking it was just another harmless prank. But panic set in as the dye began to stain their clothes and hair, and the water supply dwindled.

It wasn't until the fire department arrived, ready to declare a state of emergency that Tommy finally revealed himself. He emerged from the water tower, covered in green dye, and proclaimed himself the winner of the prank war.

The town was in chaos, but Tommy couldn't have been happier. He had pulled off the ultimate prank and knew that his reputation as the King of Deception would live on for years to come.

The end.

CHAPTER 2

A Fool and His Money

"I bet if I had a dollar for every time this automated teller machine rejected my money,

I'd have enough to buy my automated teller machine."

Story # 1

April Fools' Jokes:

1-Tell your friend you've invested all your money in a new cryptocurrency called "FoolCoin" and watch them panic.

2-Send out an email to your co-workers announcing that the company has decided to implement a new policy of mandatory clown costumes on Fridays.

3-Swap the sugar and salt containers in your house, sit back, and enjoy the reactions of your unsuspecting family members.

April Fools' Day stand-up comedy:

Hey, hey, hey! What's up, everybody? It's your favorite comedian, and tonight we'll talk about April Fools' Day when lying and deception are not only allowed but also celebrated!

So, you know what they says, "A fool and his money are soon parted." And what better day to prove that than April Fools' Day? Let's be honest; people will fall for anything on this day. You can tell them the sky is green, and they'll believe it!

And don't even get me started on all those "prank" products that people waste their hard-earned money on. Who needs a fake vomit or a whoopee cushion when you can use your natural bodily functions? Trust me; I've tried it. It's way more authentic, and it's free!

But you know what grinds my gears? Those fake lottery tickets! You know the ones where you scratch off the numbers and think you won the jackpot, but then it turns out to be a big fat joke? I mean, that isn't kind. I almost lost my best friend to one of those things.

And speaking of friends, have you ever been pranked by a loved one on April Fools' Day? I have. My girlfriend told me last year that she would have a baby. I was thrilled! But then she revealed that it was just a prank. That was a close call. I was already picking out baby names and planning the nursery.

Anyway, I hope you all have a great April Fools' Day, don't believe everything you hear, and don't spend your hard-earned money on fake gag gifts. And if you want to play a prank on someone, tell them that pineapple belongs on pizza. That's sure to get a reaction.

Thank you, and goodnight!

Story # 2

Once upon a time, a man named Bob was known for being a bit of a fool. Bob was always getting himself into trouble with his harebrained schemes and wacky ideas. One day, Bob decided he wanted to become rich, so he devised a plan to start his own business.

Bob's idea was to create a line of designer toilet paper. He thought that people would be willing to pay top dollar for something stylish and functional. So, he invested all his savings into this new venture and launched his product on April Fools' Day.

To his surprise, people started buying his designer toilet paper. They loved the unique patterns and soft texture. Bob's business started to take off, and he became a millionaire almost overnight.

However, as time passed, Bob realised he had made a colossal mistake. He had become so obsessed with making money that he had lost sight of what was truly important in life. He had no real friends, no hobbies, and no sense of purpose beyond his business.

One day, Bob woke up and decided that he had had enough. He sold his company and used the money to travel the world, try new foods, and meet new people. He learned that there was more to life than just money and success.

In the end, Bob realised he had been the biggest fool. He thought money would bring him happiness, but he was wrong. True happiness comes from living a life full of joy, love, and laughter. And that, dear friends, is no joke.

The end.

Story # 3

April Fools' Jokes:

Joke 1: Why did the rich fool fall for the April Fools' Day prank about winning a billion dollars? Because a joke and his money are easily pranked!

Joke 2: Why did the penny-pinching fool refuse to fall for any April Fools' Day pranks? Because he didn't want to risk losing even a single cent!

Joke 3: Why did the frugal fool keep all his money hidden on April Fools' Day? Because he knew the day was full of tricks, and he didn't want to be a fool with his money!

Funny Short Story:

Once upon a time, a wealthy businessman named Mr. Moneybags loved to flaunt his wealth to anyone who would listen. He drove fancy cars, wore expensive suits, and talked about his stock portfolio at every opportunity. He even had a framed copy of his bank statement hanging on the wall of his office!

One April Fools' Day, Mr. Moneybags received an email informing him that he had won a billion dollars in sweepstakes. Thrilled with his sudden windfall, he eagerly followed the instructions in the email, which directed him to wire a small processing fee to claim his prize.

Blinded by his greed, Mr. Moneybags didn't stop to think that he had never entered any sweepstakes or that the email was full of typos and grammatical errors—he wired the processing fee right away and eagerly awaited his billion-dollar payout.

Days pass, and Mr Moneybags heard nothing. He tried to contact the sweepstakes company, but the phone number and email address he had been given needed to be fixed. It wasn't until he checked his bank account that he realized he had been had - the company had taken his processing fee and disappeared.

Feeling like a fool, Mr. Moneybags was forced to swallow his pride and admit to his friends and colleagues that he had fallen for an April Fools' Day prank. He learned that sometimes, a fool and his money are easily parted - especially on April Fools' Day!

The end.

CHAPTER 3

Fool's Gold

The police were confused when they
found out the thief had stolen
a chocolate necklace

they didn't know whether to charge
him with theft or give him
a glass of milk.

Story # 1

April Fools' Jokes:

1. "What's better than fool's gold on April Fools' Day? Real gold that you give to someone as a prank, then watch as they struggle to figure out if it's a real gift or just a cruel joke."

2. "I tried to fool my friend with some fake gold, but he was too smart for me. He told me that I must have mistaken his bank account for fool's gold because it's always empty."

3. "I once gave my friend a box of fool's gold and told him it was worth millions. He believed me until he took it to a pawn shop, and they offered him a bag of peanuts in exchange for it."

April Fools' Day stand-up comedy:

Ladies and gentlemen, how are we all doing tonight? Good? Great! Well, let's get right into it, shall we?

So, April Fools' Day. It's that time of the year when we all become pranksters and jokers, and it's the one day when it's socially acceptable to lie, deceive and mislead our loved ones.

But let's be honest here folks. Some of us take this day way too seriously. How many of you have fallen victim to an April Fool prank that went too far? Get those, hands up, don't be shy.

Ah, yes, I see some of you out there. You poor, poor fools. At least you didn't fall for the classic "fool's gold" prank, right? You know the one I'm talking about, where someone puts a fake piece of gold in your hand, and tells you you've struck it rich. Yeah, that's not funny. It's mean.

But hey, if you want to pull off a good prank on April Fools' Day, you've got to put in the effort. Don't settle for fool's gold; go for the real deal. Think about how much fun it would be to trick a friend into thinking they won the lottery, only to find out it was all a joke.

Or how about pretending to be a long-lost relative who inherited a fortune and wants to share the wealth? That's the kind of prank that's worth the effort.

But seriously, folks, April Fools' Day is about having a good laugh and not taking things too seriously. So, let's all have some fun, play some pranks, and enjoy the day for what it is - a chance to be silly and laugh with our friends and family.

And if all else fails, remember the words of the great philosopher Homer Simpson: "It's not a lie if you believe it." Happy April Fools' Day, everyone!

Story # 2

Once upon a time, a small town famous for its annual April Fools' Day pranks. The town's citizens would spend months planning and preparing the most elaborate and hilarious antics to play on one another.

One year, a group of pranksters decided to pull the ultimate prank on the town. They spent weeks creating fake gold bars made of tin foil and spray-painted them to look like the real deal. On April Fools' Day, they placed the fake gold bars in various locations throughout the town, with notes attached to them that said, "Congratulations! You found fool's gold!"

The town's citizens were ecstatic when they found the fool's gold bars. They celebrated and took pictures with their newfound wealth, not realizing it was all just a prank. They even went as far as to organize a parade to showcase their newfound riches.

But as the day went on, the pranksters started to notice something strange. The town's citizens were acting more selfish and greedy than ever before. They fought over the fool's gold bars, and some even resorted to stealing them from each other.

The pranksters realized their joke had gone too far, so they decided to come clean. They revealed that the fool's gold bars were fake and apologized for causing chaos in the town.

The citizens of the town were embarrassed and ashamed of their behavior. They realized the value of April Fools' Day was not in the pranks or the material possessions, but in the joy and laughter, it brought to the community.

From that day on, the town's citizens vowed never to let a prank get the best of them again. They continued to celebrate April Fools' Day but with a newfound appreciation for the true meaning of the holiday.

The end.

Story # 3

April Fools' Jokes:

1. "To trick my friend into thinking I had given it to him on April 1st, I gave him a box of fool's gold. It turns out he's a geologist who knew it was fake immediately. I'm the absolute fool here.

2. "I got pranked on April Fools' Day with a bag of Fool's Gold. But hey, at least it's worth something to the Tooth Fairy."

3. "On April 1st, I thought I'd hit the jackpot when I discovered a massive nugget of gold in my backyard. But when I looked closer, it was just a chocolate Easter egg wrapped in gold foil. It looks like the Easter Bunny got me before April Fools' Day even started!"

Funny Short Story:

It was April Fools' Day, and the town was excited. Everyone was planning their pranks and jokes, eager to one-up each other and make their friends and family laugh. But one person in the city didn't find the holiday particularly amusing: older man Jenkins.

Jenkins was a grumpy older man who lived alone in a dilapidated house on the outskirts of town. He never participated in any of the town's festivities and certainly didn't have a sense of humor. But this year, the townsfolk decided to try to change that.

They gathered together and devised a plan to give Jenkins a taste of his medicine. They would sneak into his house in the dead of night and cover everything in tin foil. The furniture, the walls, the floor, and even his beloved cat, Mr. Whiskers, would be wrapped in shiny silver foil.

The night of April Fools' Day, the townsfolk crept up to Jenkins' house and got to work. They covered everything in sight with tin foil, giggling and whispering to each other as they worked. But as they were about to leave, they realized they had made a grave mistake—They needed to check if Jenkins was home.

They quietly pushed open the door and tiptoed inside, but to their surprise, they found Jenkins sitting in his armchair, reading a book by candlelight. He looked at them with a scowl and asked, "What in tarnation do you think you're doing in my house?"

The townsfolk stammered and tried to explain that it was just a harmless prank, but Jenkins wasn't having any of it. He stood up, grabbed a roll of tin foil from the kitchen, and started wrapping the pranksters up like burritos.

"Looks like you fellas forgot the most important rule of April Fools' Day," Jenkins said with a smirk. "Be ready to be pranked at any time."

The townsfolk laughed and admitted that the older man had outsmarted them. From that day forward, Jenkins became known as the King of April Fools' Day, and the townsfolk eagerly awaited his pranks every year. And as for Mr. Whiskers, he seemed to enjoy his new tin foil coat and wore it proudly for weeks to come.

The end.

CHAPTER 4

Fool's Luck

"Why do you have an umbrella
on a sunny day?"

"I'm a vampire.
The sun is not my friend!"

Story # 1

April Fools' Jokes:

1. You know what they say about April Fools' Day - it's the only day of the year when you can fool your boss without getting fired!

2. "On April 1, I thought I'd struck it rich when I stumbled upon a twenty dollar bill on the sidewalk, but when I went to pick it up, I discovered that it was stuck to the concrete. Talk about a sticky situation!"

3. According to what I've heard, some people like to put jelly in their coworkers' desk drawers on April 1. So I made the decision to take it and scatter it throughout my boss' office. He's having a lot of fun, let's just said, trying to get back to his desk.".

April Fools' Day stand-up comedy:

Hey, hey, hey! What's up, everyone? It's your favourite stand-up comedian, here to make you laugh, or at least try to.

So, April Fools' Day Fool's Luck, huh? What's with all the pranks and the jokes and the fake news? It's like the world trying to tell us that lying is acceptable, just as long as it's funny.

And you know what? They might be right! Who needs honesty and integrity when you can laugh at someone else's expense?

But let me tell you; there's nothing worse than being on the receiving end of an April Fools' prank. One time, my friend decided to put blue dye in my shampoo. I didn't even know until I walked around with a bluehead for a whole day! And let me tell you, no one wants to look like a Smurf on a Monday morning.

But you know what's worse than being pranked on April Fools' Day? Having nothing happen to you at all! It's like, what am I, not funny enough to be pranked? Do people not care enough about me to put in the effort? It's like I'm a comedy orphan.

And what about that whole "Fool's Luck" thing? What kind of luck is that? It's like winning the lottery, but you get a whoopee cushion and a fake spider instead of money.

It's all in good fun, right? As long as we're not hurting anyone, laughter can go a long way. And who knows maybe one day, we'll all be able to look back on those silly pranks and realize they were the best times of our lives. Or we'll be too busy trying to get the blue dye out of our hair.

Anyway, that's all for me, folks. Keep on laughing, and happy April Fools' Day!

Story # 2

It was April Fools' Day, and Tom had decided to prank his best friend, Mike. He had been planning it for weeks and was confident it would go off without a hitch.

Tom had set up a fake treasure hunt for Mike to go on, complete with clues that would lead him all around town. The final clue would lead Mike to a big box containing a huge cash prize. Of course, the cash prize was just a stack of Monopoly money, but Tom was sure that Mike would be too excited to notice.

So, on April 1, Tom left the first clue in Mike's mailbox and waited for him to take the bait. Sure enough, Mike was hooked and spent several hours running all over town, following clue after clue.

As Mike got closer and closer to the final location, he could hardly contain his excitement. He sure he was about to win big and could already picture the things he would buy with his winnings.

Finally, he arrived at the box that Tom had set up. He tore it open with a huge grin, ready to claim his prize. But when he saw the Monopoly money, his face fell.

"Tom! Mike shook his head in surprise and admitted, "You got me good.". "I can't believe I fell for it."

Tom laughed and clapped Mike on the back. "That's what friends are for, man. Happy April Fools' Day!"

The end.

Story # 3

April Fools' Jokes:

1. I tried to play a prank on my cat for April Fools' Day, but she looked at me like, "Please, I pull pranks on you every day."

2. Did you hear about the guy who tried to prank his girlfriend by pretending to propose on April Fools' Day? She said yes, but she was pranking him too - she was breaking up with him!

3. "I always thought that April Fools' Day was just an excuse for people to play pranks on each other. But then I realized that it's also a day to test your luck. I tried to win the lottery on April 1, and guess what? I won! But then the next day, I found out that my winning ticket was just part of my friend's elaborate prank. Fool's luck indeed."

Funny Short Story:

Once upon a time, a man named Jack was always down on his luck. No matter what he did, things never seemed to go his way. He was always broke, his relationships never lasted, and he could never catch a break.

One day, as he was walking down the street, he saw a sign that read, "April Fools' Day Fortune Teller - Guaranteed Fool's Luck." Jack didn't believe in fortune tellers, but he was so desperate for a change of luck that he decided to try it.

When he entered the fortune teller's tent, he was greeted by a mystical-looking woman with a crystal ball. She told him to close his eyes and make a wish. Jack wished for wealth, love, and happiness.

The fortune teller opened her eyes and said, "Congratulations, you have been blessed with fool's luck! Now everything you touch is gold."

Jack couldn't believe his luck. He left the tent and went to the nearest convenience store to buy a lottery ticket. To his surprise, he won the jackpot! He then went to a coffee shop and met the love of his life. They married the next day after falling in love.

Jack was on top of the world. He quit his job, bought a mansion, and travelled the world. But as time passed, he realised that his "fool's luck" wasn't all it was cracked up to be.

Everything he touched turned to gold, including his food, clothing, and even his wife. He couldn't hold hands with her without turning her into a gold statue. He couldn't eat without turning his food into inedible metal.

Eventually, Jack realised that true happiness couldn't be bought with money or luck—He returned to the fortune teller's tent and asked her to take back his fool's chance.

The fortune teller agreed, and Jack went back to his old life. But he was happier than ever because he had learned the value of what he had.

The end.

CHAPTER 5

Fooling the Boss

The boss enters his office and sees
a resignation letter on his desk.

Boss: Who wrote this
resignation letter?

Coworker: Oh, that's our new intern,
April Fools!

Story # 1

April Fools' Jokes:

1. "Why was the scarecrow recognised with a prize? Because he was exceptional in his choice speciality!"

2. "What caused the tomato's sudden change in color? It was drawn to the salad dressing!"

3. "How come the coffee called the police? Something happened, and it was robbed!"

Funny Short Story:

Once upon a time, a boss was known for being very serious and never cracking a smile—his employees were tired of this, so they decided to prank him for April Fools' Day.

They devised the idea of putting a whoopee cushion on his chair and replacing his usual black coffee with a bright green drink made of food coloring and lemon juice.

The following day, the boss sat at his desk, and as soon as he did, the whoopee cushion let out a loud farting noise. The boss was so surprised that he cracked a smile, and the employees couldn't believe their eyes.

The boss then took a sip of his coffee and made the funniest face ever. He spits the green liquid all over his papers, and the employees burst out laughing.

From that day on, the boss wasn't serious anymore, and the employees and boss bonded over the silly prank they had pulled.

The end.

Story # 2

At a small startup company, the employees were excited to finally be able to play a prank on their boss, who was known for his love of technology. On April Fools' Day, they decided to give him a taste of his medicine by hacking into his computer and changing all his desktop backgrounds to pictures of cats.

The boss, a self-proclaimed tech expert, was baffled when he couldn't get rid of the cute cat pictures. He tried everything he could think of, but no matter what he did, the backgrounds stayed the same.

Frustrated, the boss called IT for help, but when they arrived, they were in on the joke and told him that the only way to fix it was to watch cat videos for an hour straight. The boss is reluctantly agreed but soon found himself laughing and enjoying the silly videos.

By the end of the hour, the backgrounds had been restored, and the boss was grateful for the much-needed break from work. He thanked his employees for the prank and even admitted that he was a little bit of a cat person after all. The team was glad they could bring a smile to their boss's face and make work a little more fun.

The end.

Story # 3

In a busy marketing agency, the employees always seek ways to lighten the mood and have some fun at work. On April Fools' Day, they decided to prank their boss by sending her on a wild goose chase for a non-existent meeting.

The team created a fake email from a high-level client requesting an urgent meeting with the boss. The boss, who was always professional and never missed a meeting, quickly gathered her things and headed to the specified location.

To her surprise, the location was a park bench with a picnic basket waiting for her. The basket contained a note from her team, inviting her to join them for a lunchtime picnic. The boss was initially confused, but then she realized it was all a prank.

She joined her team on the blanket, and they all enjoyed a laugh and a delicious meal together. The boss appreciated the break from work and the chance to bond with her team. She was grateful for their creativity and sense of humor and promised to have her prank ready for next April Fools' Day.

The end.

CHAPTER 6

April Fools' Day in the Classroom

One student switches the salt
and sugar containers on the
teacher's desk.

Teacher: "I can't drink this!
It's so salty!"

Student: "Well, you'll never have to
worry about high blood pressure."

Story # 1

April Fools' Jokes:

1. Why did the student put a clock in the school's milk jug? To make April Fool's Day a daily event!

2. Why did this student bring a ladder to school on April Fool's Day? So he could reach the top of the class!

3. Why did the student put a fake spider on his teacher's desk? To see if she was arachnophobic!

Funny Short Story:

Once upon a time, it was April Fools' Day in Mrs. Johnson's classroom. The students were eager to play some pranks on each other. Little did they know, Mrs. Johnson had a surprise for them too.

As the students walked into the classroom, they noticed that their desks had been rearranged in a circle. They also saw a bucket of water hanging above the door with a string tied to it.

"Good morning, class," said Mrs Johnson. "Today, we're going to play a game. One of the first people to enter will have a bucket of water dropped on their head."

The students giggled as they tried to devise ways to avoid getting soaked. But when the bell rang, they all jumped out of their seats and rushed towards the door. They were stopped short when they saw Mrs. Johnson tied the door handle to her desk with a piece of string.

"April Fools!" she said, laughing. "Just wanted to see how quickly you could see all react."

The students were relieved that they didn't get wet, and they were impressed with Mrs. Johnson's prank. They quickly got to work on their pranks—one student placed a fake spider on another student's desk. Another student wrote a fake note from the principal, telling the class they had a surprise test that day.

As the day went on, the pranks got more elaborate. One student even brought in a whoopee cushion and placed it on Mrs. Johnson's chair. The pillow made a loud farting sound when she sat down, and the class erupted in laughter.

Mrs. Johnson was surprised but impressed. She had never seen her students so creative. As the day ended, she told the class that she was proud of them for using their imagination and making each other laugh.

"Remember," she said, "April Fools' Day is all about fooling around and playing practical jokes on one another, but it's vital never to hurt anyone's feelings."

The students agreed and walked out of the classroom, already planning their pranks for the following year.

The end.

Story # 2

It was April 1st, and the students in Mr. Smith's science class were ready for mischief. They all loved playing pranks on each other for April Fools' Day, and Mr. Smith was known for his love of practical jokes. This year was no different.

Mr. Smith told the students that they would have a pop quiz on the periodic table. The students groaned and started to panic, but Mr. Smith added, "And you'll have to answer the questions while wearing these." He pulled out a box of ridiculous-looking glasses with exaggerated nose and chin pieces. The students were shocked, but Mr. Smith laughed and said, "April Fools'!"

Next, one of the students, Tyler, decided to prank his friend Amanda. He replaced the standard light bulb in the classroom with a black light bulb, so when Amanda turned on the mornings, everything appeared to be the same, except her clothes and skin were glowing.

Another student, Emily, convinced everyone in the class that the school would have a "no-talking day." The students were so excited about the prospect of not talking for the entire day that they couldn't wait to go home and tell their families.

But the best prank of all came from Mr. Smith. He told the students that he had discovered a new planet and that they would travel there in a spaceship. The students were ecstatic and couldn't wait to embark on their intergalactic adventure.

It wasn't until the end of class that Mr. Smith revealed the truth: the spaceship was just a cardboard box with a sign that read "Don't forget to recycle." The students were disappointed but couldn't stop laughing at how they had fallen for the prank.

Ultimately, it was a fun and memorable April Fools' Day in Mr. Smith's science class, filled with laughter and good-natured pranks. The students couldn't wait for next year to come so they could play even more tricks on each other.

The end.

Story # 3

It was April Fools' Day, and Mr. Jones' science class students were ready for some hijinks. But Mr. Jones had a surprise for them. He had devised a particular experiment that would turn the tables on the students and play a prank on them.

The experiment was called "The Color-Changing Solution." Mr. Jones explained that he had mixed a unique solution that would change color when it came into contact with the skin. He then passed out the beakers of the solution to each student and told them to pour it into their hands.

As the students poured the solution into their hands, they noticed it turned bright pink. They were shocked and a little worried, but Mr. Jones assured them that it was just a harmless prank and that the solution would wash off easily.

The students were relieved but soon realized that the solution was more than just a prank. It was also a science lesson. Mr. Jones explained that the color change was caused by a chemical reaction between the solution and the oils in their skin.

By the end of the class, the students had not only had much fun but also learned about chemical reactions and the properties of solutions. And they couldn't wait to tell their friends about the prank that had turned into a science lesson.

Mr. Jones was happy that he had found a way to make science fun and engaging for his students, and he was already thinking about next year's April Fools' Day experiment.

The end.

CHAPTER 7

The Great Food Prank

A student swaps out the filling in his classmate's sandwich with toothpaste.

Student A: "What's worse than a toothpaste sandwich?"

Student B: "What?"

Student A: "A mouthwash smoothie!"

Story # 1

April Fools' Jokes:

1. I told my friend I had just discovered a new fruit that tasted like pizza. They asked me what it was called, and I said, "Pizzafruit."

2. If the cookie was so sick, why did it visit the doctor? Since it felt so brittle and fragile.

3. I told my coworkers that I brought them doughnuts, but when they arrived, it was just sliced bread with sprinkles.

Funny Short Story:

Once upon a time, there were two best friends, Jack and Jill. They were always up for a good laugh and loved to play pranks on each other.

One April Fools' Day, Jack came up with the ultimate prank. He told Jill that he had invented a new food that tasted like anything she wanted it to. All she had to do was imagine the taste, and it would come to life.

Jill was sceptical but couldn't resist the challenge. She closed her eyes and imagined a juicy cheeseburger. To her surprise, when she took a bite of the food; it tasted like a cheeseburger!

Jill was amazed and couldn't wait to try more. She imagined a slice of pizza and then ice cream, and the food transformed to match her thoughts each time.

However, when she tried to imagine something healthy, like a salad, the food tasted like junk food. That's when she realized that Jack had tricked her and filled the food with junk food all along.

Jill couldn't stop laughing and thought it was the best April Fools' prank ever. From then on, every April Fools' Day, Jack and Jill would play a food-themed joke on each other and enjoy a good laugh.

The end.

Story # 2

Once upon a time, a group of coworkers loved to play pranks on each other. One day, one of them had an idea for the ultimate food prank—They decided to swap all the sugar in the office kitchen with salt.

The next day, everyone in the office started making their morning coffee and grabbing snacks from the kitchen. At first, everything tasted fine, but after a few sips and bites, they all realised something was off. Everything was much saltier than usual!

Panic quickly spread as people started questioning what was happening with the food. Then, one of the coworkers who were in on the prank announced that it was April Fools' Day and revealed the truth about the salt in the sugar.

Everyone had a good laugh, and from that day on, the coworkers checked their food and drinks carefully on April Fools' Day. The person who came up with the prank was crowned the office prankster for the year, and everyone was already excited to see what they would come up with next year.

The end.

Story # 3

Once upon a time, a group of friends loved to play pranks on each other. One April Fools' Day, they decided to do a massive food prank.

The first friend brought in a bowl of what appeared to be cereal made of mashed potatoes. The second friend brought in a "cake" made of blended vegetables. The third friend brought in a "juice" that was just a mixture of mustard and vinegar.

As the day went on, the pranks became more and more elaborate. One friend convinced the others that they were eating a new type of meat made from rubber bands!

But the best prank came from the final friend, who brought in a "pie" filled with whipped cream and whoopee cushions. When they all took a bite, they were surprised by the loud farting sounds!

Everyone laughed and realised they had all fallen for The Great Food Prank. They enjoyed the rest of the day playing more pranks on each other and munching on real food. And they all lived happily ever after, looking for their next prank opportunity.

The end.

CHAPTER 8

When Pranks Go Wrong

A couple tells their friends and family that they're having a baby, only to reveal that it was all a prank and they're getting a puppy.

"I can't wait to see your baby bump!"

"Thanks, but I think you mean puppy bump."

Story # 1

April Fools' Jokes:

1. When I was younger, I learned to play the piano by ear, but I use my hands these days.

2. Why don't scientists trust atoms? Because they make up everything!

3. I told my wife that his brows were too high. She couldn't believe it.

Funny Short Story:

A group of friends once took great joy in pulling practical jokes on one another. One April Fools' Day, one of them decided to play a mark on the rest of the group by putting a whoopee cushion on each of their chairs.

However, things turned wrong when one of the friends sat on a cushion that was a little too powerful, causing him to fly out of his chair and into the air. He landed with a thud on the floor, breaking his arm.

The group quickly realized their prank had gone wrong and rushed their friend to the hospital. After getting his arm treated, the friend forgave them, and they all laughed about the incident.

From that day forward, they made a pact to play pranks that wouldn't harm or injure. And they all lived happily ever after, laughing and enjoying each other's company without mishaps.

Moral of the story: When playing pranks, ensure they are harmless and don't harm or injure others.

Story # 2

A group of coworkers once loved to play pranks on each other. One April Fools' Day, one of them decided to put a fake spider in their boss's office.

However, things quickly worsened when their boss, who had a severe fear of spiders, walked into the office and spotted the fake spider. In a panic, she ran out of the office and into the streets, causing a commotion and disrupting the entire office building.

The coworkers soon realized that their prank had gone too far and that their boss was scared and extremely upset with them. They apologized to their boss to make things right and promised never to play such a mean-spirited prank again.

From that day forward, the coworkers made a pact only to play pranks that were light-hearted and wouldn't cause any harm or embarrassment to anyone. And they all worked happily ever after, enjoying each other's company and the occasional harmless prank.

Moral of the story: When playing pranks, ensure they are in good fun and don't cause harm or embarrassment to others.

Story # 3

Once upon a time, a group of friends loved to play pranks on each other. One April Fools' Day, one of Jake's friends decided to play a joke on his best friend, Sam. He convinced Sam that he had won the lottery and was now a millionaire. Sam was ecstatic and couldn't believe his luck.

Jake then took it a step further and convinced Sam to go and buy a new car, telling him that as a millionaire, he deserved the best. Sam went and purchased a brand new sports car and was so excited to show it off to his friends.

But when he arrived back at their meeting place, the rest of the group revealed to Sam that it was all a prank. Sam was devastated and felt like a fool. He had spent all his savings on a car he didn't need.

Feeling guilty, Jake decided to make it up to Sam. He secretly entered him into a real lottery, and a few weeks later, Sam found out that he had won a large sum of money.

From that day on, the group of friends stopped playing pranks on each other and instead focused on spreading joy and positivity. And Sam was able to keep his brand-new sports car!

The end.

CHAPTER 9

Fooling Your Friends and Family

A person is holding a box of chocolate. The person asks their friend, "Hey, want a chocolate?"

A person revealed the chocolate was a piece of soap and said, "Sorry, I couldn't resist!"

Story # 1

April Fools' Jokes:

1. Tell your friends you've decided to live as a unicorn and see how long it takes them to believe you.

2. Tell your family that you've been hired as an astronaut and will be travelling to Mars for the following year.

3. Please change the language settings on someone's phone to a language they don't know and watch the confusion.

4. Put clear tape over the bottom of a computer mouse so it can't be used.

5. Put salt in the sugar jar and see who falls for it.

Funny Short Story:

One April Fools' Day, Jack decided to prank his best friend, Jim. He told Jim that he had won the lottery and would use the money to buy a private island. Jim was so excited for Jack; he couldn't believe it! Jack told him he would fly to the island the next day for a tour.

The next day, Jack picked Jim up from his house and drove him to a remote countryside area. They got out of the car, and Jack led Jim to a tree in the middle of a field. Jack grinned and told Jim, "This is your little island."

Jim did not understand, "Just what exactly do you mean? That's just a tree in the middle of a field."

"Well, it's a special tree," replied Jack. "It's a money tree. All you have to do is shake it, and money will fall out."

Jim was sceptical but went along with it and started shaking the tree. Suddenly, a bucket of water was dumped on his head from above! Jack had climbed the tree and filled a pail with water to leave on his friend.

Jim was soaked and angry at first, but then he laughed. He realized he had been had and was a victim of an April Fools' Day prank. From that day on, the two made it a tradition to pull a trick on each other every April Fools' Day.

The end.

Story # 2

It was April Fools' Day, and Sarah had been planning her prank for weeks. She convinced her little sister, Emily, that their parents had bought a pet unicorn.

In the morning, Sarah told Emily she had a surprise for her. She brought her to the backyard, where a beautiful unicorn was waiting for her. Emily was thrilled and couldn't believe her parents had gotten her a pet unicorn.

But as she approached the unicorn, it started to make strange noises and act a little weird. Emily was a little apprehensive, but Sarah assured her it was just a silly April Fools' Day prank.

The unicorn transformed into a giant inflatable unicorn that Sarah had set up in the yard. Emily was laughing so hard that she fell to the ground. Sarah joined in, and they spent the rest of the day laughing and playing with the inflatable unicorn.

From that day on, Sarah and Emily made it a tradition to play an April Fools' Day prank on each other, and they always had a great time.

The end.

Story # 3

April Fools' Jokes:

1. Tell them you have just won the lottery and will quit your job.

2. Say that you have just adopted a giraffe, and it will live with you.

3. Tell your parents that you're going to run away to join the circus.

4. Convince your siblings that you have a superpower and can control their minds.

Funny Short Story:

Once upon a time, a naughty man named Mike loved playing pranks on April Fools' Day. He would spend the entire year experimenting with elaborate schemes to fool his friends and family.

One year, Mike chose to tease his close friend, Bob. He informed Bob they would take off that day since he had won a free ticket to the moon. Being a vast space lover, Bob was giddy with delight.

Mike then convinced Bob to put on a bulky space suit and climb into a makeshift spaceship he had set up in his backyard. Bob, being completely fooled, eagerly complied. Mike then counted down from 10 and launched the spacecraft with a loud explosion, sending Bob soaring into the air.

Bob was flying high, shouting with excitement, when suddenly, Mike jumped out from behind a nearby tree and yelled, "April Fools!" Bob was so surprised that he tumbled out of the spaceship and landed in a heap on the ground.

Although Bob was shaken up, he couldn't help but laugh at the joke. From that day forward, Bob made it his mission to play the best April Fools' joke on Mike the following year.

And so, the friendly rivalry between Mike and Bob continued, year after year, as they tried to outdo each other with the most creative and hilarious pranks.

The end.

CHAPTER 10

The Technology Trick

A group of friends are playing a game on their phones, and suddenly the screen goes black.

They panic until a message appears that says, "April fools! Your phone's battery is dead!"

Story # 1

April Fools' Jokes:

1. Why did the computer go to the doctor? Because it had a virus!

2. Why did the smartphone cross the road? To get to the App Store!

3. Why did the robot feel cold? Because it left its microchip in the freezer!

Funny Short Story:
"The Technology Trick"

They were friends who used to take great pleasure in pulling pranks on one another. One April Fools' Day, they decided to pull a trick on their friend Mike, who was obsessed with technology.

The friends went to Mike's house early in the morning while he was still sleeping and switched out his smartphone with an old flip phone. They also replaced his smartwatch with a cheap analogue watch and hid all his high-tech gadgets.

When Mike woke up and tried to use his phone, he was confused. He thought he had lost all of his technology. He spent the whole day searching for his missing gadgets and became increasingly frustrated as the day went on.

Finally, the friends revealed their prank to Mike and showed him where they had hidden his technology. Mike was relieved and laughed at the silly trick.

From that day on, Mike never took his technology for granted and always kept a closer eye on it. And every April Fools' Day, the friends would play another harmless trick on each other, keeping their friendship strong and their sense of humor intact. The end.

Story # 2

Funny Short Story:
"The Tech Swap"

One day, two friends named Tim and Dave decided to prank each other for April Fools' Day. Tim was an avid gamer, while Dave was a tech geek who loved to tinker with gadgets.

Tim came up with the idea to swap their devices. He took Dave's high-tech smartphone and replaced it with an essential flip phone, while Dave took Tim's gaming laptop and replaced it with an old, outdated desktop computer.

The following day, Tim was confused when he couldn't find his laptop. He searched all over the house, but it was nowhere to be found. However, Dave was equally puzzled when he couldn't get his smartphone to work. He tried every button, but nothing seemed to be working.

When they finally did figure out what had happened later that day, they started laughing uncontrollably. Tim was shocked at how much he struggled to play his games on the old desktop, while Dave was amazed at how much he missed all the features of his smartphone.

After a day of struggling, they finally swapped back their devices and laughed about the silly prank they had pulled on each other. From that day on, they made a vow always to have each other's back and never underestimate the power of technology.

The end.

Story # 3

Funny Short Story:
"The Great Tech Scavenger Hunt"

It was April Fools' Day, and a group of friends decided to prank their tech-savvy friend, Sarah. They created a scavenger hunt that would lead her to her missing gadgets.

The first clue led Sarah to her living room, where she found a note attached to her TV remote—the letter instructed her to search for her next clue in the kitchen. In the kitchen, she found another note attached to her coffee maker. This continued for several more clues until she finally arrived at the the last clue, which was hidden in the backyard.

When Sarah arrived in the backyard, she was greeted with a table full of all her missing gadgets, including her smartphone, tablet, and laptop. The friends had set up a fake crime scene, complete with phoney police tape, to make it look like the gadgets had been stolen.

At first, Sarah was worried, but then she saw her friends hiding behind a bush and laughing. They revealed their prank and Sarah couldn't help but laugh with them.

From that day on, Sarah always kept an extra eye on her gadgets, especially on April Fools' Day. And every year, her friends would come up with a new and creative prank, keeping the tradition alive and their friendship strong.

The end.

www.ingramcontent.com/pod-product-compliance
Lightning Source LLC
Chambersburg PA
CBHW050806160726
48004CB00002B/721